# GEORGE, THOMAS, AND ABE!

## The Step into Reading Presidents Story Collection

Photograph credit: The White House, pp. 9, 57, 105

*George Washington and the General's Dog* text copyright © 2002 by Frank Murphy,
illustrations copyright © 2002 by Richard Walz; *Thomas Jefferson's Feast* text copyright
© 2003 by Frank Murphy, illustrations copyright © 2003 by Richard Walz; *Abe Lincoln's Hat*
text copyright © 1994 by Martha Brenner, illustrations copyright © 1994 by Donald Cook

Step into Reading, Random House, and the Random House colophon are registered trademarks
of Random House, Inc.

Visit us on the Web!
StepIntoReading.com
randomhouse.com/kids

Educators and librarians, for a variety of teaching tools, visit us at RHTeachersLibrarians.com

Library of Congress Cataloging-in-Publication Data for these titles is available upon request.
*George Washington and the General's Dog*
ISBN 978-0-375-81015-2 (trade) — ISBN 978-0-375-91015-9 (lib. bdg.)
*Thomas Jefferson's Feast*
ISBN 978-0-375-82289-6 (trade) — ISBN 978-0-375-92289-3 (lib. bdg.)
*Abe Lincoln's Hat*
ISBN 978-0-679-84977-3 (trade) — ISBN 978-0-679-94977-0 (lib. bdg.)

ISBN 978-0-449-81288-4
Printed in the United States of America
10 9 8 7 6 5 4 3 2 1

# Dear Parent:

Congratulations! Your child is taking the first steps on an exciting journey. The destination? Independent reading!

**STEP INTO READING**® will help your child get there. The program offers five steps to reading success. Each step includes fun stories and colorful art. There are also Step into Reading Sticker Books, Step into Reading Math Readers, Step into Reading Phonics Readers, Step into Reading Write-In Readers, and Step into Reading Phonics Boxed Sets—a complete literacy program with something to interest every child.

## Learning to Read, Step by Step!

**Ready to Read**   **Preschool–Kindergarten**
• big type and easy words • rhyme and rhythm • picture clues
For children who know the alphabet and are eager to begin reading.

**Reading with Help**   **Preschool–Grade 1**
• basic vocabulary • short sentences • simple stories
For children who recognize familiar words and sound out new words with help.

**Reading on Your Own**   **Grades 1–3**
• engaging characters • easy-to-follow plots • popular topics
For children who are ready to read on their own.

**Reading Paragraphs**   **Grades 2–3**
• challenging vocabulary • short paragraphs • exciting stories
For newly independent readers who read simple sentences with confidence.

**Ready for Chapters**   **Grades 2–4**
• chapters • longer paragraphs • full-color art
For children who want to take the plunge into chapter books but still like colorful pictures.

**STEP INTO READING**® is designed to give every child a successful reading experience. The grade levels are only guides. Children can progress through the steps at their own speed, developing confidence in their reading, no matter what their grade.

Remember, a lifetime love of reading starts with a single step!

STEP INTO READING

# GEORGE, THOMAS, AND ABE!

## The Step into Reading Presidents Story Collection

Step 3 and Step 4 Books
A Collection of Three Early Readers

Random House · New York

# Contents

Which U.S. president:
Had a pet named Sweetlips?
Fought in the American Revolution?
And stopped a battle to help a lost dog?
Turn the page to find out. . . .

*For my father—*
*like Washington, so brave and so honest*
*—F.M.*

*For Tom and Marianne—*
*wonderful people, wonderful friends*
*—R.W.*

Author acknowledgments: *Thanks to the world's greatest librarian, Liz Dobuski, for guiding me toward this story. Thanks to Caprice Serafine for her help with mastiffs. Thanks to my editor, Shana Corey, for her grace and expertise in helping to draft this story. Thanks to Diane Landolf for help with photo research. Much of the research that went into crafting this story was supported by the words of George Washington himself through his voluminous writings, available at the Library of Congress, and by James Thomas Flexner's biography* Washington: The Indispensable Man.

STEP INTO READING®

STEP 3

# George Washington
## ✦ and the ✦
# General's Dog

by Frank Murphy
illustrated by Richard Walz

Random House 🏠 New York

1732-1799

George Washington is one of
America's greatest heroes.
Most people know that
George was honest and brave.
But there is something
about George that people
don't always know.

George Washington *loved* animals.

George learned
to ride horses as a boy.
Sometimes he rode into town.
George rode fast,
but he never fell.
People said
he was the best rider
they had ever seen.

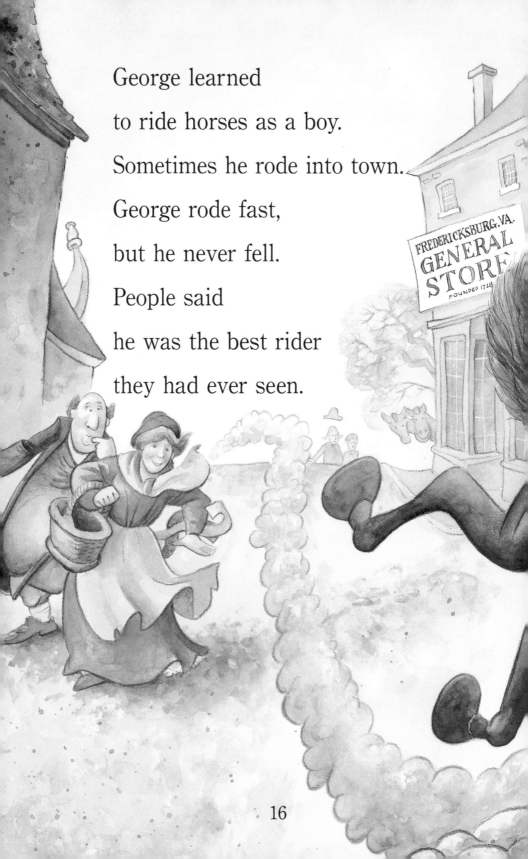

When George grew up,
he moved to a farm
called Mount Vernon.
Every day,
George checked on
the horses and hogs.

He checked on the oxen,
mules, and sheep.

But he spent the most
time with his dogs.

George had a *lot* of dogs.

He owned thirty-six dogs

in his lifetime.

He took them hunting.

He played with them.

He even gave them cute names

like "Mopsey," "Sweetlips,"

and "Truelove."

Sometimes George
spoiled his dogs.
He let them run
around the house.
One day,
George's wife, Martha,
cooked a ham for dinner.

George's dog Vulcan
jumped up and
stole the ham—
right off the table!
Martha chased after him.
But George just laughed.

George liked being
at Mount Vernon
with Martha and the animals.
But America needed him.

America was not yet

its own country.

It was an English colony.

That means it belonged

to England.

Many American colonists

wanted to be free

from England.

So they went to war.

The war was called

the American Revolution.

The colonists chose George

to be their general.

George chose his favorite dog,

Sweetlips, to go with him.

He said goodbye

to Martha and Mount Vernon.

He jumped on

his horse, Nelson.

Then he rode into battle.

Sweetlips was right beside him.

In George's day,
soldiers often brought
dogs with them to war.
Dogs helped hunt.

Dogs helped track the way.

Dogs helped guard
against wild animals.

Best of all,
dogs were great partners!

The general of
the English army
was named William Howe.
He had a dog, too.
He also had 9,000 soldiers.
They had plenty of supplies.

George did not have
nearly as many supplies.
Sometimes his soldiers
were cold.
Sometimes they were hungry.
But they did not give up.

In the fall of 1777,
George's troops
went to Pennsylvania.
They were fighting
the English troops.
Guns fired!
RAT-A-TAT-TAT!
Cannons roared.
BOOM! BANG!
Smoke filled the air.

Finally, the fighting ended.
The English soldiers
went back to their camp.
The battle was over
for the day.

The smoke began to clear.
George noticed a dog
without a soldier.
It looked lost.
George bent down
and patted the dog's head.

The dog followed George
back to the colonists' camp.
He wagged his tail.
*Whose dog is this?*
wondered George.

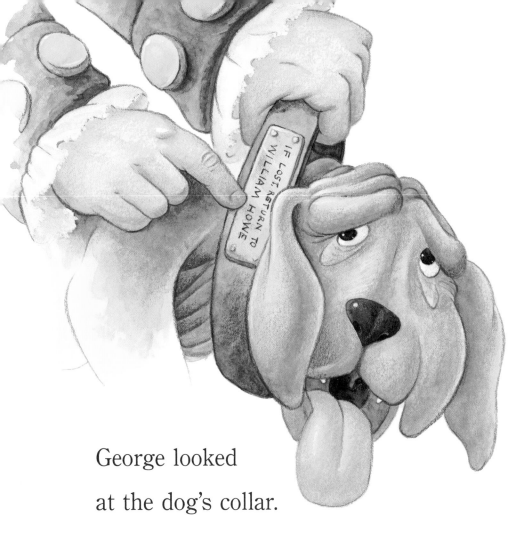

George looked

at the dog's collar.

The tag had

a man's name on it.

That name was William Howe.

*William Howe!?*

George couldn't believe his eyes!

William Howe was the enemy!

Word about the enemy dog
spread through camp.
Some of George's men
wanted to keep the dog.
But George said no!
George believed the dog
belonged with his master.
George had his friend
Alexander Hamilton
write a note to General Howe.
The note said that George
wanted to return the dog.

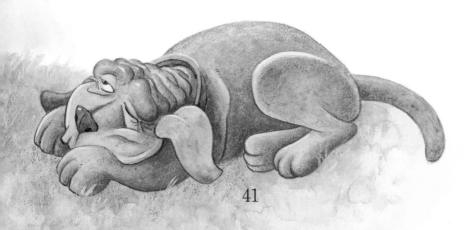

Both sides raised white flags.
The white flags meant
no one could fight.
George's soldiers
walked the dog
across the battlefield.

They gave him back
to General Howe.

People in England
found out about
George's good deed.
The English still wanted
to beat George
and win the war.
But now they respected him.
Some English people
even liked him.
They had never heard
a story of such great kindness
between enemies.

In 1783, America won
the war against England.
America became
its very own country.
George Washington
went home to Mount Vernon.

Friends around the world
wanted to honor George.
They wondered what
he would like.
Then they remembered
the story about the dog.
Soon, presents started
arriving at Mount Vernon.

The King of Spain
sent George a mule!
George named him
"Royal Gift."

A friend from France gave George
an even bigger gift—
seven dogs!

FROM
MARQUIS DE
LAFAYETTE
TO
GEORGE WASHINGTON
MT. VERNON
VIRGINIA

George's work
was not done, though.
The American people
needed a leader.
They elected George
to be their first president.

People all over America
loved their new president.
They cheered when
he rode by in his carriage.
They knew it was him
because his six white horses
always led the way.

# AUTHOR'S NOTE

The stories in this book are true. We can't be sure *exactly* how they all happened, but we've tried our best to show the way things might have been.

Alexander Hamilton

George Washington with Nelson

William Howe

George Washington's actual letter to General Howe. It says, *"General Washington's compliments to General Howe, does himself the pleasure to return him a Dog, which accidentally fell into his hands, and by the inscription on the collar, appears to belong to General Howe."*

Which U.S. president:
Wrote over 20,000 letters in his lifetime?
Made his own ice cream?
And brought French fries to America?
Turn the page to find out. . . .

*For Katie Claire Gisondi and Jack Gisondi,*
*two unforgettable little treats*
*—F.M.*

*To Mary, with love*
*—R.W.*

Author acknowledgments: *Thanks to Bryan Craig, research librarian at Monticello, for his expertise. Thanks to my talented editor and collaborator, Shana Corey, for her patience and creativity. Thanks to Angela Roberts for her assistance. And thanks to Mark Klein for finding that apple picker!*

Photograph credits: Portrait of Thomas Jefferson: © Burstein Collection/CORBIS. Macaroni-making machine courtesy of the Library of Congress.

# Thomas Jefferson's
## FEAST

by Frank Murphy
illustrated by Richard Walz

Random House 🏠 New York

Long ago, before your great-great-grandparents were born, there lived a man named Thomas Jefferson. You probably know his name because he was the third president of the United States.

But that's not all there is to know about Thomas Jefferson.

Thomas Jefferson loved to read.

He collected books about the stars and books about history. In fact, he had one of the largest libraries in America.

Thomas Jefferson also loved to write.

He wrote letters to people like Benjamin Franklin and George Washington. In his lifetime, he wrote over *20,000* letters. That's like writing a letter a day, every day, for 55 years!

Many of Thomas's letters said that America should be its own country. (The British thought America belonged to them.)

So Thomas Jefferson went to work writing the Declaration of Independence. He wrote and rewrote it for 17 days straight—until he got it just right.

Of course, with all that reading and writing and thinking, sometimes Thomas Jefferson got tired.

Sometimes his back hurt.

And sometimes he got hungry. When that happened . . .

. . . he usually took a break and had a snack. Because Thomas Jefferson really, *really* loved food!

Thomas liked food *so* much, he
sometimes spent as much as 50 dollars
on groceries in just one day! (That would
be like spending *750* dollars today!)

Thomas also spent a lot of time *thinking* about food. He even thought about better ways to get food!

Sometimes Thomas Jefferson got hungry late at night after everyone else had gone to bed.

When that happened, he had to tiptoe down the hallway and all the way downstairs to the kitchen.

Then he had to fix a tray of food and carry it *all* the way back upstairs and down the long, dark hallway to the dining room.

If he was lucky, there was still a little left when he sat down to eat.

Thomas needed an easier way to get his food upstairs.

So he built a little elevator in his house. It was too small to carry people. But it could take food and drinks from the kitchen to the dining room upstairs—without spilling a drop! Thomas called his invention a dumbwaiter.

Thomas's dumbwaiter is still in his house in Virginia today—and it *still* works!

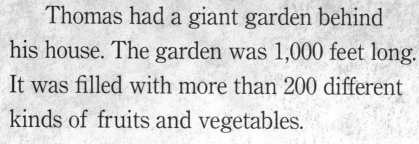

Thomas had a giant garden behind
his house. The garden was 1,000 feet long.
It was filled with more than 200 different
kinds of fruits and vegetables.

If you visit Thomas's house, Monticello, today, you can still see many of the fruit trees he planted.

Sometimes Thomas wanted a snack from his garden. But the apples on the bottoms of the trees were usually already picked.

"Hmmm," thought Thomas. "There must be a simple way to get apples from the tops of the trees."

Thomas found a long wooden pole. He attached a metal basket to it. The basket had hooks at the top.

He used the hooks to pull off the apples. Presto! Ripe apples fell into the basket!

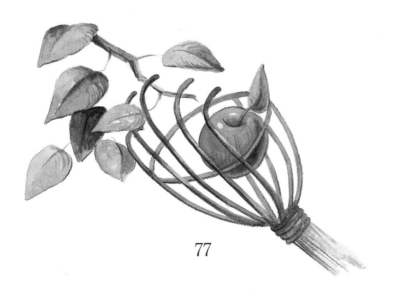

In 1784, Thomas sailed to France. He wanted to help make America's friendship with France stronger.

Thomas was sad to leave America and Monticello. But he knew it was an important job. He also knew there would be *lots* of new foods to try!

Thomas was right!

In between meetings, he tasted macaroni covered with cheese!

He munched on potatoes fried in the
French manner.

One night, he went to a dinner party.

"Hello!" said Thomas.

"*Bonjour!*" said his host. (*Bonjour* means "hello" in French.)

Thomas's host offered him a special dessert. It was ice cream wrapped in a warm pie crust. Ice cream hadn't come to America yet.

For *bonjour*, say: bohn-JOOR

Thomas took a bite.

"Good!" said Thomas.

"*Bon!*" said his host. (*Bon* means "good" in French.)

For *bon*, say: bohn

During his visit, Thomas saw a
Frenchman eating a bright red fruit.
It was called a *pomme d'amour.* (That
means "love apple" in French.) Thomas
had seen the fruit before. But in America
it was usually just used for decoration.
Most people thought it was poison, so no
one ate it.

The Frenchman promised it was not
poison. So Thomas took a bite.

Thomas *loved* the love apple!

For *pomme d'amour,* say: pohm dah-MOOR

Thomas stayed in France for five years. When it was time for him to go back to America, he couldn't wait to share all his new favorite foods!

He wrote down the recipes for macaroni and cheese, fried potatoes, and ice cream. He even decided to plant some love apples at Monticello.

He waved goodbye to his French friends and got on the ship.

"*Au revoir!*" he said. (*Au revoir* means "goodbye" in French.)

For *au revoir,* say: oh ruh-VWAHR

"How was France?" everyone asked when Thomas got home.

"Delicious!" answered Thomas.

He decided to have a feast to show off the new foods.

Of course, that was easier said than
done.

Thomas planted love apple seeds—

and waited for them to grow.

He drew a picture of a macaroni-making machine he had seen in France. Then he sent a friend all the way to Italy to buy one. (Thomas had heard that Italy had the best macaroni-making machines!)

He dug up potatoes from his garden.

Finally, he made ice cream. This was *not* easy. First he mixed cream and eggs and sugar. He packed it with ice and salt.

Then he stirred and stirred *and stirred*.

At last, everything was ready. The love apples were ripe. The macaroni was cheesy. The potatoes were crisp. The ice cream was icy.

"Perfect!" said Thomas.

Thomas invited all his friends.

"What's for dinner?" they asked.

"It's a surprise," said Thomas. "Let's eat!"

Thomas's guests loved the feast! They gobbled up the macaroni and cheese. They ate every last fried potato. They asked for more of Thomas's ice cream. They even asked for the recipes.

When they were about to go home,
Thomas noticed something. No one had
touched their love apples! Everyone
believed they were poison.

"Try them," Thomas begged.

"No thanks," everyone said. "We're full."

Thomas felt terrible! How could he get
people to try love apples?

The next day Thomas rode into the town of Lynchburg to visit a friend. He noticed a few love apples growing in her yard. Suddenly, Thomas had an idea!

He asked if he could pick a few love apples. His friend said yes.

Thomas walked down the street with the love apples.

He raised one to his mouth. People stopped and pointed. "What are you doing?" they shouted. "That's poison! Stop!"

Thomas took a bite.

"Oh no!" everyone said. "Save him! He's going to get sick!"

But Thomas didn't get sick.

He just kept eating.

Pretty soon, people got curious
about the love apples. They tried them
themselves. *"Scrumptious!"* everyone said.

And to this day, Americans enjoy eating
love apples. (Especially on pizza!)

Today, we still eat many of the foods Thomas Jefferson brought from France. Only now we call "potatoes fried in the French manner" French fries. And we call love apples tomatoes!

(Macaroni and cheese is still called macaroni and cheese, and ice cream is still called ice cream!)

# AUTHOR'S NOTE

Thomas Jefferson stayed in France from 1784 to 1789. He may not have served all the foods in this book at one party. But he really did introduce them to America. And he was well known for his fancy dinner parties. So it just may have happened this way.

Thomas Jefferson also really did have a pet mockingbird that flew around his study. His name was Dick.

*Thomas Jefferson*

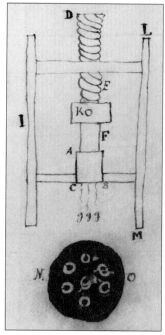

*Thomas Jefferson's drawing of a macaroni-making machine*

Which U.S. president:
Rode a horse named Old Buck?
Liked a good practical joke?
And was more than a little forgetful?
Turn the page to find out. . . .

*For Daniel and David*
*—M.B.*

Photograph credits: Duff Armstrong: Lincoln's New State Historic Site and the Illinois Historic Preservation Agency; Stephen Douglas, Abraham Lincoln, Judge Davis: Illinois State Historical Society, Springfield, Illinois.

# Abe Lincoln's Hat

by Martha Brenner
illustrated by Donald Cook

Random House 🏠 New York

Abe Lincoln didn't have much money.
But when he became a lawyer,
he wanted to look his best.
He bought a long black coat
and a tall black hat.

Every day Abe wore his hat

to his new job.

People noticed the tall man

in the tall hat.

He was friendly to everyone.

When they needed a lawyer,

they remembered him.

Abe lived in Illinois.

His state was mostly wilderness.

Then more and more settlers came.

They built houses and farms
and new towns.

Sometimes they didn't get along.

They argued over land
and animals and money.
Lawyers like Abe could help people
settle their arguments.
They could help people get
a fair trial in court.

Abe Lincoln was a smart lawyer.

People came to him

with all kinds of problems.

He helped them all.

But he had one problem himself.

He forgot to answer letters.

He forgot where

he put important papers.

A good lawyer cannot forget.

Abe wanted to be a good lawyer,

but he was not a good paper-keeper.

What could he do?

Abe had an idea.

His tall hat!

He could push letters deep inside it.

He could stuff notes

into the leather band.

When he took off his hat,

the papers would remind him

what he had to do.

The idea worked, most of the time.

One day some boys

played a trick on Abe.

They tied a string across the street.

They strung it way up high.

Everyone in town could walk under it.

Everyone except Abe.

When Abe walked down the street,

the string knocked off his hat.

Papers flew everywhere!

He bent over to pick them up.

The boys ran out of hiding.

They jumped all over him.

Abe laughed.

He was not mad at the boys.

He liked a good joke.

But the trick did not stop him

from carrying papers in his hat!

Once a lawyer sent Abe a letter.

Abe stuck it in his hat.

The next day, Abe bought a new hat.

He put away his old one.

Weeks later the lawyer wrote again:

"Why didn't you answer my letter?"

Then Abe remembered.

The letter was still in his old hat!

Many towns in Illinois
had no lawyers and no judges.
So every spring and fall,
a judge and some lawyers traveled
from town to town.
Abe went too.
He packed his hat with papers,
his checkbook, and a handkerchief.

At the head of the parade
of lawyers rode the judge.
No one could miss him.
He weighed over 300 pounds.
Two horses pulled his buggy.

Abe's horse was skinny and slow.

His name was Old Buck.

Abe and Old Buck traveled

lonely country roads.

In the snow.

In the rain.

In the mud.

Traveling made Abe very tired.

He dreamed of a soft bed

and a good meal.

But the lawyers had to stay

at poor country inns.

The food was bad.

The rooms were cold.

The beds were crawling with bugs.

The lawyers had to share beds.

Except the judge.

He had his own bed.

Early in the morning

the courthouse bell would ring.

Abe hurried to court.

Pigs lived under one courthouse.

Abe had to talk loudly

over the grunts and squeals.

People came from near and far

to hear Abe.

He made trials easy to understand.

He told jokes and stories.

People said he could make a cat laugh.

Once Abe whispered a joke
to another lawyer.
The lawyer laughed out loud.
"Quiet!" the judge yelled.
"You are fined five dollars."

When the trial was over,

the judge asked to hear the joke.

He laughed as hard as the lawyer.

"That was worth five dollars," he said.

"Forget the fine."

At another trial

two men argued

over who owned a young horse.

Each said he owned

the mother of the colt.

Abe led everyone outside.

He put the two grown horses

on one side of the lawn.

He held the colt on the other side.

Then he set the colt free.

It headed straight to its real mother!

One day Abe got a letter.

It was from Hannah Armstrong.

Years before, Abe had lived
with her family.

Mrs. Armstrong cooked for Abe.

She sewed up the holes in his pants.

Now she begged Abe for help.

Her son Duff was in jail—for murder!

Abe did not stick this letter in his hat.

He wrote back right away:

"Of course I'll help you."

Duff had been in a big fight.

It was very dark.

But a man said

he saw Duff

kill someone.

Duff said he did not do it.

Abe believed Duff.

But how could he prove that

the man was wrong—

or lying?

"How could you see in the dark?"

Abe asked the man.

"The moon was full," the man said.

"It was bright as day."

"Are you sure the moon was full?"

Abe asked again and again.

"Yes," the man repeated.

Then Abe held up
a famous book of facts.
It said there was NO moon
in the sky at the time of the fight!
Now no one believed
the man anymore.
The judge set Duff free!

Abe believed slavery was wrong.

His state had laws against it.

But the laws were not clear.

Many blacks were treated like slaves.

Nance was one of them.

She worked for a storekeeper
who sold her to another man.
This man treated Nance badly.
So she would not work for him.

Abe argued for Nance in court.
Illinois was a free state, he said.
All its people were free,
whatever their color.
The judge decided Abe was right.
From then on, no one could be
bought or sold in Illinois.

Abe had saved Nance.

But half the states in America
still had slaves.

In a few years there would be
new states out west.

Abe did not want slavery to spread
to these states.

Abe tried to get elected
to the U.S. Senate.
If he won, he could make laws
to stop slavery.
He ran against Stephen Douglas.
Douglas argued that each state should
decide for itself if it wanted slaves.
They gave speeches all over Illinois.
Thousands of people heard them.
Abe lost the election but became famous.

In 1860, Abe ran for president.

Stephen Douglas ran too.

This time Abe won.

Abe grew a beard for his new job.

He took his family to Washington.

At every train station,

crowds cheered the new president.

Abe was ready to make
his first speech as president.
He carried a cane, a tall silk hat,
and his speech.
He looked for a place
to put his hat.
Stephen Douglas stepped up.
"If I can't be president," he said,
"I can at least hold his hat."

Abe Lincoln was a great president.

He freed the slaves.

He worked for fair laws.

He helped unite the nation

after a long war.

But he never changed his ways.
He always kept important papers
in his tall hat!

Judge David Davis

Duff Armstrong

Stephen Douglas

Abraham Lincoln

All the stories in this book are true and
all the people really lived. Here are photos
of some of them. When the photos were taken,
around 1860, the camera was a new invention.

# Looking for other exciting, inspiring true stories? Try these Step into Reading titles:

BABE RUTH SAVES BASEBALL!

BARACK OBAMA:
OUT OF MANY, ONE

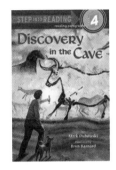

BEN FRANKLIN AND
THE MAGIC SQUARES

THE BRAVEST DOG EVER:
THE TRUE STORY OF BALTO

CHRISTOPHER COLUMBUS

DISCOVERY IN THE CAVE

EAT MY DUST!
HENRY FORD'S FIRST RACE

ESCAPE NORTH! THE STORY
OF HARRIET TUBMAN

FAIRIES! A *TRUE* STORY

THE FIRST THANKSGIVING

FRANCIS SCOTT KEY'S
STAR-SPANGLED BANNER

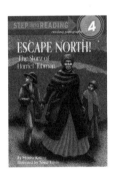

THE GREAT HOUDINI:
WORLD-FAMOUS MAGICIAN
AND ESCAPE ARTIST

HELEN KELLER:
COURAGE IN THE DARK

ICE MUMMY

LEWIS AND CLARK: A PRAIRIE
DOG FOR THE PRESIDENT

LISTEN UP! ALEXANDER GRAHAM
BELL'S TALKING MACHINE

LOOKING FOR BIGFOOT

POMPEII . . . BURIED ALIVE!

THE *TITANIC:*
LOST . . . AND FOUND

THE TRUE STORY OF
POCAHONTAS

TUT'S MUMMY:
LOST . . . AND FOUND

# If you like true animal stories, you won't want to miss . . .

Nothing the musher did could get the dog to move forward. . . . The musher had seen this sort of behavior before. He knew exactly why neither dog would lead. They could no longer pick up the trail through the high winds and blowing snow.

In other words, they were lost.

Then, in his position close to the rear, Balto strained in his harness and barked. Still crouching by the unmoving lead dog, Kaasen turned to look at Balto. He could barely see through the haze of snow, but Balto's body language was clear. *He* knew which way to go. *He* knew the trail!

# The true story of Ernest Shackleton's exciting Antarctic adventure!

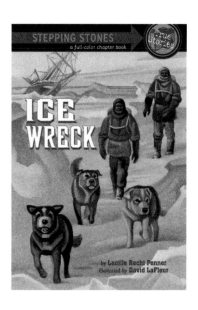

All around them, the ice rocked and trembled. The *Endurance* sprang leaks. Everyone worked to pump out the water. Some of the men jumped over the side and hacked at the ice with shovels and axes. But it was no use. The ice was too thick to scrape away. Then a huge piece of ice ripped a hole in the side of their ship. Water poured in. The *Endurance* was breaking up. Soon it was going to sink.

Sadly, Shackleton gave the order.

*Abandon ship.*

## If you like exciting true stories, you won't want to miss . . .

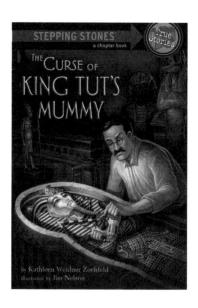

Carter made the hole a little wider and stuck the candle through it. He peered in. Lord Carnarvon and Lady Evelyn stood anxiously by his side. Carter was silent. His eyes got used to the dim light. Then beautiful forms began to take shape. "Strange animals, statues, and gold—everywhere the glint of gold."

Lord Carnarvon couldn't wait any longer. "Can you see anything?" he cried.

It was all Carter could do to get out the words. "Yes, wonderful things!"